INFINITE GIVING

The 7 Principles of Givers Gain®

Authors: Ivan Misner, Ph.D., Greg Davies, Julian Lewis

Editors: Heidi Scott Giusto, Ph.D.

Cover Design: Ashley Misner, Olivia Pro Design

Layout Design: Lyubomyr Yatsyk

Giver's Gain® is a registered trademark of BNI and is used with permission.

For more information on other books visit:
http://www.IvanMisner.com.

TABLE OF CONTENTS

INFINITE GIVING
PROLOGUE

From our experience in the networking organization BNI, we have learned that Givers Gain®, the principle core value of the organization, can make a huge difference in people's success. We've written this book based on these experiences in BNI; however, we believe that these experiences translate into many different aspects of networking and more importantly, life in general. Our goal for this book is to lay out the 7 Principles of Givers Gain and how someone can apply them to their business and to their life.

Givers Gain is more than a phrase—it's a way of living one's life. It's a perspective to view and interact with the world. It's an attitude, not an expectation. When it's applied properly, it will change your life and when it changes enough lives, it will change the world.

Givers Gain is more than a phrase—it's a way of living one's life. It's a perspective to view and interact with the world. It's an attitude, not an expectation. When it's applied properly, it will change your life and when it changes enough lives, it will change the world.

STYLE COMMENT

This book was written by two Brits and a Yank. We loved working together. It was a great experience. However, we did run into a conundrum that we could not resolve; do we use Queen's English or American English?

So, in true democratic fashion, we flipped a coin.

The Yank won.

For the rest of the English-speaking world, we would like to apologize or apologise, whichever you prefer.

Dr. Ivan Misner (The Yank)
Greg Davies (The Brit)
Julian Lewis (The Brit)

CHAPTER 1

WHY INFINITE GIVING?

On Friday May 11, 2018, James, dressed in brown suit trousers, a cream shirt, and a brown striped tie, sat down on a donation chair, which was immediately tilted backward by a nurse into a reclined position.

He rolled up his right sleeve, stretched out his arm, and allowed the application of a combined tourniquet and blood pressure collar. Once all the checks were done, a clear antiseptic solution was spread over the targeted vein and a large bore needle was inserted to allow the donation to begin.

James winced as the needle entered his arm, not from the pain of the entry itself, but due to the combination of the stinging from the antiseptic and a long-held aversion to needles. The clear tube attached to the needle began to fill with blood, and the donation began.

If you've ever given blood, this sounds like a pretty standard scenario, but there were a few things different about the appointment.

James was 81 years old, and under normal circumstances, he shouldn't be there. At the time, he was a full one year and five months over the Australian National Health Service's (ANHS) upper age limit for donating blood.

Second, there was a crowd of people who had gathered to watch James donate. It's commonly agreed that donating blood is one of the most philanthropic things you can do, however, a spectator sport it is not.

The final abnormality was four giant silver foil balloons anchored to the floor and floating at eye level behind James's head.

This event had drawn quite a crowd. The room was full of smiling doctors, nurses, politicians, journalists, and parents holding newborns who were more interested in the camera flashes bouncing off of the meter-high 1173 shaped balloons than they were in the grey-haired man in the chair.

This man was James Harrison, the "man with the golden arm," and, as reported in both the *New York Times* and the *Daily Telegraph* this was his 1173rd and final blood donation.

In 1954 at the age of 18, James started donating blood. Soon after, he learned of an anomaly in his blood: it contained a high concentration of antibodies that fought the D Rh group antigen. This powerful discovery, and James's commitment to donating, ultimately enabled research scientists to use the antibodies to develop an immune globulin product that was, in turn, used to prevent haemolytic disease of the newborn (HDN), a serious and potentially fatal disease.

These products containing a high level of anti-D antibodies were given to mothers and babies during and after pregnancy to prevent the formation of Rhesus disease.

So unique was his blood and considered so important, James's life was insured for $1 million AUD after this discovery. Research based on his donations led to the creation of the commercially available anti-D immunoglobulin known as RhoGAM.

James has been credited with saving over 2.4 million babies, a feat made possible by donating plasma, on average, once every three weeks for over 60 years.

On James's 808th donation, the Guinness World Records recognized him as the most prolific donator of all time. James, when speaking about his achievement said "If you can't take 10 minutes to give a unit of blood and it can save and help so many people, then that's the most worthy thing, I think, that anybody can achieve."

On the day of his last donation, James massaged a red piece of glossy foam between the fingers of his right hand and cheerfully answered questions from journalists while a young couple carried their daughter across to his chair. Dressed in a pink onesie with a hair band to match, the young girl immediately poked James in the eye, which only served to widen the smile on his face. She had no comprehension of the lifesaving gift that this man has bestowed on her.

James's story is a great example of someone who, for decades, put himself through discomfort for the benefit of others, but James is not our only hero of this story.

The people we should also be recognizing are the many donors that made up the 13 liters of blood that James received when he underwent lifesaving chest surgery at the age of 14.

> **In the coming chapters, we'll introduce, explore, and reinforce the principles behind Givers Gain, and how, if embraced in life and in business, it can have profound effects on all aspects of society, leading to Infinite Giving.**

As he lay in his hospital recovery bed, the realization of these people's selfless act began to dawn on him and he pledged to begin donating as soon as he turned 18, at the time, the lower age limit for the ANHS.

The story of James Harrison exemplifies the concept of this book. In the coming chapters, we'll introduce, explore, and reinforce the principles behind Givers Gain, and how, if embraced in life and in business, it can have profound effects on all aspects of society, leading to Infinite Giving.

This karmic activity is something that most have undertaken, experienced, and benefitted from. With some understanding and application, Givers Gain could easily change the world.

As for James, you may be thinking that his Givers Gain was transactional and weighted heavily in our favor. However, that's not how Givers Gain works. Tracey Mellowship, James's daughter, received RhoGAM during her pregnancies. In James's attempt to honor the gift that he had received when just 14 years old, he had saved millions of children, but by far, to him, the two most cherished were his two grandsons who would not be with him today if not for the creation of the RhoGAM.

Givers Gain is not a commodity that can be spent or traded.

Scott Mellowship, the youngest of James's grandsons, donated for the first time on the same day that his grandfather gave his 1000th. Scott was just 16, now the lower age limit for blood donation in Australia.

Givers Gain is not a commodity that can be spent or traded. It is not finite. When applied with intent, it will lead to Infinite Giving, a karmic force that will continue to influence those that experience it for as long as we recognize, respect, and nurture its principles.

The law of cause and effect is about the way we can influence people around us through our actions and our behaviors. When those actions and behaviors are about helping people, we've learned that truly amazing things are possible.

We are going to break down Givers Gain into composite parts and introduce the seven key principles that, when applied properly to those around you, create Infinite Giving.

By living a life of Givers Gain, you will benefit from the transcendent force—actions that when combined become more than the sum of their parts and rise above and beyond their original purpose and ultimately become Infinite Giving.

Throughout this book we have used the expressions Givers Gain, the 7 Principles of Givers Gain, and Infinite Giving to describe the transformational power of giving. It has been said to us that at times the phrases Givers Gain and Infinite Giving seem interchangeable. Therefore, we have created a simple formula to explain how they are different and why they need each other to work.

Givers Gain is a philosophy. The 7 Principles of Givers Gain is the codification of how to make Givers Gain work for everybody and become Infinite Giving.

An easy way to remember how all these ideas fit together is to consider this formula:

Givers Gain plus the 7 Principles equals Infinite Giving, or:

$$GG + 7P = IG$$

This book is about how the philosophy of Givers Gain can change the world.

By implementing the ideas in this book, we know, like the people in James's story, you'll have your gift of giving returned many times over.

This book is about how the philosophy of Givers Gain can change the world.

CHAPTER 2

THE ORIGIN OF GIVERS GAIN

To make your time investment in this book worthwhile, we need to establish the origin story of Givers Gain.

Givers Gain allows for both giving and receiving. It is the yin and yang of the business world.

It is a two-sided concept that is very different from pure philanthropy, which is normally practiced by incredibly wealthy business magnates who realize they need to give something back to the world to secure a legacy. So, they go about building libraries, universities, theatres, and hospitals or embarking on a quest to right one of the world's wrongs as they see it at the time.

Givers Gain allows for both giving and receiving. It is the yin and yang of the business world and was born, like most great things, out of necessity.

In 1984, a management consultant had just spent a year developing and training a sales department for his largest client, a newly formed computer sales company. His success had allowed him to take a step up the property ladder and afford a large mortgage with a larger monthly payment.

Despite the success of this new department, which was now generating significant revenue for his client, when it came around to his contract being renewed, against all expectation and for reasons beyond his cause or control, the relationship was terminated. It turns out the client was woefully underfunded and needed to reduce expenses dramatically.

This left the management consultant in a difficult position because approximately half of his revenue was directly attributed to this client, causing problems to his cashflow. Despite his training and ability, he was adamant that cold calling, while effective, was the single most soul-destroying way of generating business. He knew that he did not want to employ this method to replace his now absent client.

After analyzing his remaining customers, he could see that all his clients either came from public speaking engagements or from referrals. He set about doing two things:

First, he hit the rubber chicken circuit (it's called the rubber chicken circuit because of the quality of the mass-catered meals). Over the course of the next 12 months, he spoke at more than 120 community service groups to increase his exposure and profile with the goal of generating more referrals. Second, he set out to find a networking group that had the system and structure in place to generate high-quality referrals.

The first was easy; there are always groups looking for confident speakers who are knowledgeable about their chosen subjects. The second, however, proved to be more of an issue.

At the time, two types of networking groups existed:

mercenary and social. And for very different reasons, neither of these effectively generated the type of business that he was seeking.

The mercenary groups were all about transactional relationships—they were about selling, selling, selling, selling, where the only real focus was finding out where you kept your wallet and how to pry it open before the time was done. Most business owners have experienced them. They were the kind of group that you went to and felt "slimed," like you needed a shower when you got home to cleanse yourself of the culture of the meeting. He valued relationships, and these groups had no focus on those.

What I need is a network of people I trust.

The social groups were all about Happy Hour and hors d'oeuvres—the participants didn't even wear name badges. These groups consisted of a cross-section of people who felt like they needed to be seen and those who just wanted to mix and mingle. Our protagonist didn't want to make friends. Rather, he wanted to do business with people that he liked. At one of the more social events, he recalls someone saying to him, out of the corner of their mouth, "If I wanted a friend, I'd buy a dog. What I need is a network of people I trust."

He also valued business opportunities, and these groups had

no structure in place to allow the proper business relationships to flourish that would ultimately lead to referrals being passed.

Neither group served business well, so he decided to merge the two extremes and form a third, more effective type of group in 1985. This new group would have the focus on business, without being mercenary, and the focus on social while also allowing it to be more relational.

The glue that would bind this new type of group together would be the concept of Givers Gain, the idea that if I help you, you'll help me, and we'll all do better as a result of it. This was a much more relational approach to networking than the more common transactional approach to the process.

Originally called The Network and now known as BNI (Business Network International), today, you can walk into any one of the thousands of chapters in dozens of countries and ask the membership, "What is the philosophy of BNI?" In resounding chorus, the response will come bouncing back, "Givers Gain!"

While this unified response alone is an amazing achievement, we doubt there is any other organization in the world where, without fail, every single one of their customers could recite the corporate philosophy. This law of reciprocity has allowed hundreds of thousands of people to take part in a philanthropic activity while also building a business to support them and those around them.

If we respect the principles of Givers Gain, it has the potential to change the world, full stop.

Givers Gain was born out of the need to find a better way of working together and has ultimately changed the way the world does business. More than that, if we respect the principles of Givers Gain, it has the potential to change the world, full stop.

Oh, and we are honored to say that the management consultant in question is one of the co-authors of this book Dr. Ivan Misner, the father of modern networking (and it's not Ivan writing this part of the book).

CHAPTER 3

GIVING IN THE MODERN WORLD

We get it. Some of you are sitting there thinking that this karmic approach to life and business has no place in the modern world and the thing is, you wouldn't be alone.

Whether you're a Boomer, Gen X, Millennial, or Gen Z, you have been surrounded by movies like Wall Street, Glengarry Glen Ross, and Wolf of Wall Street. These movies tell us that success in business is coming to terms with asking yourself the question, "can you afford to take lunch?" because "lunch is for wimps!"

Many sales directors even today are still telling their young recruits that success is putting your competition in the ground, and for you to get a sale it MUST mean that someone else loses out—and the sales directors believe that is OK.

This approach is problematic. While modern media has idolized and sometimes satirized some of the stories from the past, it has ignored those who have fallen victim to stresses of constant isolation and competition.

Humans are inherently pack animals. We will always seek out an opportunity to be part of something more than ourselves; it is our natural default. In the wonderful words of sixteenth-century poet John Donne:

> No man is an island entire of itself; every man
> is a piece of the continent, a part of the main;
> if a clod be washed away by the sea, Europe
> is the less.

The Hollywood approach to business does not allow for us to consider anyone other than ourselves, and, while there have been outliers who have achieved huge financial gains, we ignore those who have failed or burned-out along the way.

Even Jordan Belfort, the "Wolf of Wall Street," now earns money from sharing lessons of his ultimate failure and admits when speaking about his Wall Street days that "my greatest regret is losing people's money."

Infinite Giving allows us to enjoy the connection to others that we yearn for. It gives us the opportunity to contribute to and share success.

How do we apply this to business?

At its basic level, it is about picking a core value that ultimately benefits others, shouting about it, and sticking to it. There is of course a little more to it than that, which we will explore as we go through the book. This could be something simple like sourcing materials locally, using only recyclable packaging, or joining with other small businesses to help one another grow.

One of the best viral pictures of the last five years, now replicated almost daily on a sign or notice board, was an image of a chalkboard stating: "When you buy from a small business, you're not helping a CEO buy a third holiday home. You are helping a little girl get dance lessons, a little boy get his team jersey, a mom and dad put food on the table. Thanks for shopping local."

We are sure you have seen a version of this around a holiday or shared by a friend on social media. It's a very powerful and thought-provoking concept that taps into our modern morals.

However, and of somewhat of a side note, it is still only one of our favorite chalkboards of all time. We all agree that the top spot should be reserved for one seen outside of a pub in the middle of the countryside in West Sussex, England. It read, *"Customers Wanted, Apply Within."*

Genius.

While there will always be those who are cynical about the idea of karmic capital, the concept of what goes around comes around, there will also be those who insist we can do more. These people will have a strong set of values at the heart of what they do, and from values morals are born. Having a strong moral code is the foundation for success.

Having a strong moral code is the foundation for success.

Such success is evident in the popular shoe brand TOMS and its founder Blake Mycoskie. In 2002 Blake and Paige Mycoskie placed third in Season 2 of *The Amazing Race*, missing out on the $1 million prize by just four minutes. During the race, which lasted for over two months, the pair spent a short amount of time in South America.

Blake wanted to revisit the continent and in 2006 arrived in Argentina. During his vacation, he met an American woman who was part of a volunteer organization that provided shoes for children, the lack of which is often a barrier to education, employment, and breaking the cycle of poverty.

Blake spent several days with the charity, travelling from village to village helping with their life-changing efforts. However, there was a problem. Truckloads of donated secondhand shoes would turn up to be distributed and more often than not, the majority of the shoes would not be given to those who needed them. They were the wrong size, not fit for purpose, or not in good enough condition.

Inspired, Blake founded TOMS, the "For-Profit built on Karmic Capital" shoe company, and created and embraced the One for One™ philosophy. For every pair of shoes they sold to a standard consumer, they would donate a brand new pair to a child that needed them from a developing nation.

It seems like such a simple concept: build a business on a strong moral foundation and allow the owners, investors, workers, and those less fortunate to benefit. Why doesn't everyone do it?

We find it sad that most people tend to sit on the sidelines rather than get involved, and even Blake has a few trolls out there who suggest that instead of providing these life changing gifts, he should just "send them the money." This also makes us think of a powerful quote by Teddy Roosevelt about the hard and valuable work of being dedicated to a cause:

> It is not the critic who counts; not the man who points out how the strong man stumbles, or where the doer of deeds could have done them better. The credit belongs to the man who is actually in the arena, whose face is marred by dust and sweat and blood; who strives valiantly; who errs, who comes short again and again, because there is no effort without error and shortcoming; but who does actually strive to do the deeds; who knows great enthusiasms, the great devotions; who spends himself in a worthy cause; who at the best knows in the end the triumph of high achievement, and who at the worst, if he fails, at least fails while daring greatly, so that his place shall never be with those cold and timid souls who neither know victory nor defeat.

If you have an idea to help others, please act upon it. It could grow into something amazing and, at the very least, you'll make a difference to those around you. Don't worry about those who do not have the foresight that you hold; no statue has ever been built for a critic.

As for Blake, described as the most relaxed, intense person you'll ever meet, he will be comforted by the fact that his idea has provided almost 100 million pairs of new shoes, in the correct size, to those that need them most and has allowed the charity TOMS supports to move into other vital areas lacking in developing nations, such as eyecare.

A great way to help yourself is to help others.

Embracing Infinite Giving is not only vital for your business, your customer, and supplier loyalty, but also for your own well-being. We cannot imagine anyone laying on their deathbed wishing that they had made just one more sale; however, knowing that we have supported others is a comforting thought that will never lose its impact.

A great way to help yourself is to help others.

CHAPTER 4

THE 7 PRINCIPLES OF GIVERS GAIN

The 7 Principles of Givers Gain
lead to a life of Infinite Giving.

People who live Givers Gain believe that the world is a better place when our first thought is to give. We codified the 7 Principles of Givers Gain in this book as a way of putting structure around a philosophy designed to help people who wish to adopt the concept and use it to its full potential. The principles are the result of the combined experience of the authors, and they build upon our thoughts and subsequent decades of implementing the concept.

The 7 Principles of Givers Gain lead to a life of Infinite Giving.

Givers Gain starts with us all taking personal responsibility for our own actions in the context of the 7 Principles, which will lead to a personal life of Infinite Giving.

Givers Gain is an elegant and simple phrase that people can unite behind both personally and as a group. Its simplicity is its power as with lots of great philosophies of life. Because it is so simple, it opens itself up to wild interpretation by those who hear it. Yet when left totally unchecked, simplicity can get corrupted and misinterpreted. When this happens the value and power of the philosophy is reduced both personally and collectively. The 7 Principles are designed to magnify the positive effect of the philosophy of Givers Gain.

Givers Gain starts with us all taking personal responsibility for our own actions in the context of the 7 Principles, which will lead to a personal life of Infinite Giving. Once we have set the standard for ourselves, we can then move on to our wider community in ever increasing circles.

In addition to creating a much bigger impact on the world through Givers Gain, the principles introduce some new elements to the philosophy that allow it to move beyond its beginnings in BNI and into the global population with structure and purpose. One such element is the idea of Givers Gain Communities.

Givers Gain Communities are distinct groups of people who have a strong connection with each other and to the philosophy of Givers Gain. Givers Gain Communities started in BNI. The 7 Principles of Givers Gain allow many diverse groups of people to adopt Givers Gain as a philosophy in life and business. These communities, whether a part of BNI or not, can use these principles to ensure that their giving and the benefits derived from giving are sustainable forever.

Typically, Givers Gain Communities will share a purpose. Below are examples of such communities.

1. Families
2. Business groups
3. Sports teams and their supporters
4. Religious groups
5. Political groups
6. Shared interest clubs and societies
7. Individual businesses
8. Friendship groups
9. Educational groups (schools, colleges, and universities)
10. Neighborhood groups

When people in these communities understand the power of Givers Gain, they can use the principles to ensure that their giving is appropriate and sustainable. Let's look at the following example.

Dino Tudisca was asked to take part in the TV show Extreme Makeover Home Addition by a member of his business group that had only formed the year before.

Dino rallied the other members of the group and got behind this project wholeheartedly. Many members of the group invested time, energy, and resources over the coming months and made the project a reality. Dino, himself, was the project manager for the build. The group made a tangible difference in their local community by embracing Givers Gain.

Because Givers Gain isn't finite, its infinite, the initial energy invested has perpetuated. Dino has now worked on several projects for the show, with the most memorable being in Joplin, Missouri, where they helped rebuild a whole community of tornado-damaged homes.

But the most impactful reward for Dino came in the form of a surrogate brother named Lucas who was 12 years old when Dino helped rebuild his home. They are now the closest of friends. Dino says, "It is true when we put the needs of others above our own personal desires, we gain experiences that money cannot buy. We become rich in so many ways."

The 7 Principles also introduce the concept of fairness and equality to Givers Gain. If abused, the philosophy can be manipulated to gain but not to give by people with low levels of integrity. On the flip side to that, some people spend so much energy in giving that their gain fails to meet their basic needs, and this can cause them hardship. Once everyone has adopted the principles of Givers Gain, then the whole world can both give and gain in a way that is viewed as fair in a modern society.

The principles are also there to protect active members of our Givers Gain Communities. We've seen people who have stepped away from a group or community without feeling the full benefit of Infinite Giving. It's often accompanied by the phrase, "they just didn't get it."

What we realized was, is that what they didn't get was that there were steps that had to be taken and principles that had to be applied before they could really become a part of the Givers Gain Community.

The 7 Principles of Givers Gain are a guide to obtaining and sustaining the wonderful concept of Infinite Giving. They are also a check and measure for every aspect ensuring that people maintain harmony in their lives.

Givers Gain seeks to imagine a world where diversity is a strength, and everybody can create success.

We do, however, understand that, on a global scale, there will always be imbalance. Some people with have more resources than others. Givers Gain seeks to imagine a world where diversity is a strength, and everybody can create success. Givers Gain is simply a philosophy that says if I give to you then you will be motivated to give to me or others within our Givers Gain Community. If enough people do this within the boundaries of the 7 Principles of Givers Gain, then communities around the world will be in a better place. We will achieve a world where everyone can thrive in line with their talent and as a result of their hard work.

We explain the 7 Principles using the experience of the authors of how people can implement a sustainable Givers

Gain strategy. When Givers Gain is understood well, people can adopt the philosophy as a way of life, and they can spread the word in their own communities and make the world not just a better place but also a nicer place.

Givers Gain has both a practical and a psychological effect in how communities see themselves. Givers Gain Communities are positive places to live, so much so that Givers Gain both attracts positivity and reduces the number of negative actions and thoughts in any community.

The next chapters outline the 7 Principles of Givers Gain. It is those principles that drive Infinite Giving and when adopted people, communities, and businesses will thrive.

The 7 Principles of Givers Gain

1. Are They in Your Light?
2. Give Without Expectation.
3. Give More Than Expected.
4. Give What You Can Afford.
5. It's OK to Gain.
6. Stay Humble.
7. Show Gratitude.

Giving will only be sustainable when the principles are applied in full and the process of Infinite Giving can begin. Let's move into the first principle.

CHAPTER 5

PRINCIPLE 1, ARE THEY IN YOUR LIGHT?

Life is about discernment.

Infinite Giving begins with this important principle. Think of a really large room, and in the center of the room is a single light hanging down from a wire. Standing under that light—is you. All around you are people who are close to you, important to you, or just simply hanging around you. A little further out are people you can talk to, but who are not directly in the glow of your orb. Further still are people you can see but can't really talk to easily. In the dark corners of the room are people who are long forgotten, or maybe even placed there on purpose.

Life is about discernment. Sometimes that discernment includes evaluating the people in your life and how they impact your personal and professional environment. This principle asks you to evaluate how people are positioned around you in life. Are they in the dark corners of your room, are they directly under the light, or are they somewhere in between? The concept is based, in part, on the book, *Who's in Your Room?* by Misner, Emery, and Sapio.

Imagine that you live your life in one room and that room has only one door and that one door is an "Enter Only" door. When people come into your room and into your life—they are there forever; you can never get them out! You may think this is a metaphor, but it's actually more than that. The authors explain why in their book. One of their critical lessons is that the quality of your room depends upon the people in your room.

"I don't want you hanging around little Johnny. He's a bad influence." Remember your Mom (or another adult) saying something like this to you when you were growing up? We do. What we didn't know at the time was that it would apply to us for the rest of our lives!

Infinite Giving does not mean you should be an infinite victim.

This is where discernment comes into play. Infinite Giving does not mean you should be an infinite victim. If you give, and give, and give some more and end up feeling like you're a victim because people are *only taking*, then you need to be more discerning in whom you associate with. It's important to assess the people trying to gain entry into your room, or if they are in there already, assess the people who are trying to get close to you and stand under your light.

We recently received a message from someone who understood this completely. Most importantly, she came up with an idea to deal with the person effectively:

I have a toxic acquaintance whom I couldn't easily avoid. She manages to ruin every occasion for which she is present. I looked hard at how she managed this, and I realized that she threw an emotional grenade into the room just to get a reaction. If we didn't give her a reaction, then that grenade didn't explode. Each time she did what she always did, we ignored it and started to talk about something else entirely. She was furious and eventually stopped throwing the grenades, and she actually stepped back from us, allowing us to be together in peace.

The lesson here is don't feed other people's need to create chaos or to not give back to the relationship in some positive way. The world is full of givers AND takers. *Apply contextual insight and use appropriate judgment* to give freely to the people who value this positive approach to life. Use discernment for the ones who do not.

Sometimes the need for discernment applies to people who aren't toxic, but who are just not holding up their end of the relationship. In this case, be strategic in the way you handle the situation.

We know one man who gave a half a dozen referrals to someone in his networking group over the past 18 months, but the individual never reciprocated. The man came to us and asked for advice. We coached him to do the following:

Invite the person out for a one-to-one meeting and come to the meeting prepared with as much detail as possible about the six referrals you gave your contact. Start with the oldest and ask how that worked out? Did it turn into business? If so, was it as much as you had hoped? Did the relationship work out well? Use open-ended questions to determine how well that referral worked out for the individual. After a few minutes, do the same for the next one. And then the next one and so on, until you discuss all of the referrals you've given that individual.

Here is where your discernment needs to be fine-tuned. What if all those referrals you gave the individual did not work out like you thought? Then, you need to ask the person how you could give better referrals in the future. However, if any of those referrals turned out to be good and possibly resulted in business, take a different tack. Tell the person that you are really glad the referrals you gave to him worked out well. Then pause a moment and say, "Since some of them worked out well for you, I'd really appreciate if we could talk about how you might be able to give me some referrals as well. Maybe we could talk a little bit about how I can help you do that." From there, talk to the person about what a good referral is for you, how they can refer people to you, and even dive deeper into specific clients they may have who may be a good referral for you.

After the person we coached had his meeting, he came back to us and said he was so glad he followed our advice, rather than just end the relationship. He told us the individual "apologized profusely and recognized that this needed to be a two-way relationship. We spoke at length about how he could reciprocate, and he has already done so. The referral he just gave me turned into a big client!"

Sometimes, people are so busy in life, they are just not thinking about the importance of having a "reciprocal" relationship. Sometimes they don't know how, and sometimes they don't care. All three perspectives require discernment, and that discernment requires a different response strategy.

The people in our lives determine the quality of our lives.

Yes, Mom got it right. The people in our lives determine the quality of our lives. We want to reframe that slightly and say that the people in our "light" play an even bigger role in our lives. Through the concept of Infinite Giving, we want to talk about those people who are in your room who are "front and center" under the light versus those who are in the far corners of your room and no longer play a starring role. In other words, we want to talk about the people who are in your light, as well as the people who you recognize "should" be in your light, but for whatever reason, are not currently.

More of your giving energy should be focused on people

closer to your light, as these folks will be more aligned with your values. Give to them, and you will either get back more of that giving energy and motivation, or not; and now you'll have the discernment to know how to deal with them effectively.

The more energy you have for giving, the more you are able to give. Giving more where you have strong relationships makes you able to practice Infinite Giving.

CHAPTER 6

PRINCIPLE 2, GIVE WITHOUT EXPECTATION

The second principle is simple: When we give, we should do so with no expectation of any direct return on our giving. A gift is not a gift if we expect something in return. Once there is any expectation of something in return then it is a transaction.

**A gift is not a gift if we expect
something in return.**

Any individual act of giving is simply a gift. In a world where we have a mindset of Infinite Giving, which is supported by the seven principles, it is enough to know that if I apply the concept then by giving I will gain at some stage in the future. I may not yet have any idea what that gain might be, but I continue to give without expectation in the knowledge that Givers Gain.

This is the principle that most people think they understand as soon as they hear of the philosophy of Givers Gain. However, it's true to say that while people feel they understand it, this principle gets corrupted into other meanings.

**There is a difference between the long-term
strategy of a reciprocal relationship and the
transactional strategy of "this for that."**

Have you ever heard people say, "Well, I gave you that so I expect that at some stage in the future you will reciprocate?" For instance, we invited you for dinner and at some stage we expect the invite back. People do this "matching" activity all the time. Matching is not Givers Gain. There is a difference between the long-term strategy of a reciprocal relationship and the transactional strategy of "this for that."

Givers Gain works best where there is no transactional expectation.

Givers Gain is based on the principle of social reciprocity. If I give to someone then they will pay the giving forward to the community. It IS true that if I give to you then you will be motivated to return the gesture of a gift. This reality sometimes masks the second principle of Givers Gain. It gets misunderstood because we do give and get in symbiotic partnerships. When this happens a lot, we start to believe that this is how Givers Gain works. Givers Gain works best where there is no transactional expectation.

In practice, it extends well beyond the business community. We can look to everyday citizens to see how a philosophy of giving can reap deep rewards and create immeasurable positive change. In 2010, Hollywood actor Kiefer Sutherland stood at a podium at the CNN Hero Awards. With cameras trained upon him, his job was to introduce the film clip that outlined the next recipient of the honor.

Kiefer commented on the devastation that most people have seen at some point, whether it was a homeless woman with her children or a man literally starving on the streets. He proceeded to mention that, for most of us, we continue to go about our lives after taking a moment to regroup. He then mentioned, "But thank God there are people on this planet like Narayanan Krishnan who cannot."

Narayanan Krishnan's story is one most won't easily forget. Even though he was an accomplished chef working at a luxury hotel who been shortlisted for his dream job at a five-star restaurant in Switzerland, he made a choice to dedicate himself to helping the people of from his hometown of Madurai, Tamil Nadu, India after observing shocking poverty during a walk.

During this walk he came across an elderly man lying on the side of the road. "I saw a very old man eating his own human waste for food," Narayanan said. "It really hurt me so much. I was literally shocked for a second. After that, I started feeding that man and decided this is what I should do the rest of my lifetime."

Narayanan decided that helping this man and others in need would be a life well-lived.

He quit his career as a leading chef and began supplying meals to the homeless in Madurai. Though many of the people helped by Narayanan need much more than a meal, it was a good place to start and utilizing his own personal savings, Narayanan fed around 30 people.

He has since gone on to serve freshly cooked meals to over 1.7 million people through the formation of a charitable trust.

But it's not just meals.

> I cut their hair. I give them a shave. I give them a bath. For them to feel, psychologically, that they are also human beings, there are people to care for them. They have a hand to hold, hope to live. Food is one part. Love is another part. So, the food will give them physical nutrition. The love and affection which you show will give them mental nutrition . . .
>
> Everybody has got five liters of blood. I'm just a human being. For me, everybody's the same. What is the ultimate purpose of life? It's to give. Start giving. See the joy of giving.

Narayanan has travelled the world due to his decision, and he has been recognized with humanitarian awards and given the opportunity to speak on TED stages. However, his closing line when accepting the CNN Heroes award shows the true value of giving without expectation: "This is the right path I have taken. The people I feed are my friends and bring my inner joy … Clarity and focus are needed to know our destination. I know mine. I will continue to go to the streets again and feed these people because they need us."

When you give without expectation the "Gain" is often not related to the "Give," and for Narayanan it was something he could not achieve on his own, inner joy.

Narayanan had no expectation of fame or wealth when he used his own money to feed the first few people. He understood that giving should never be used to manipulate or motivate a desired result that benefits the giver.

Far too often people calculate that if I give something then I will get something in return that will be to my benefit. This type of manipulative thinking only has a limited ability to influence people. It breaks down the philosophy of Givers Gain and the commitment to practice Infinite Giving. Once a person realizes that an individual manipulated them with a gift, all future gifts will be either refused or viewed with skepticism.

Unfortunately, the Givers Gain concept is abused from time to time. The entire concept gets misused when we start pointing a finger at others and saying things like, "Milton doesn't have a Givers Gain attitude—he's going about things all wrong." What's interesting is that when we say things like this about other people, it's often because they're not doing something we think they ought to be doing in business or life.

To reiterate, Givers Gain is not a stick to wave around at

people who aren't doing what we think they should be doing. It is a standard we must apply to ourselves and ourselves only. Ironically, when we point our index finger at someone else, there are three fingers pointing back at us—it's a perfect reminder of whose actions and tactics we really need to be worrying about, don't you think? Don't be the person who tends to blame others for their woes instead of focusing on their own behavior.

People who criticize and point fingers at others can be caustic, which is one of the reasons it is important to be really selective about the people you surround yourself with. That said, there will undoubtedly still be people in our lives who are unendingly critical, judgmental, and just plain vitriolic. They're the people who love to *talk about you,* but who never actually *talk to you* about issues.

The 7 Principles when followed correctly allow the world to create Givers Gain Communities that sustain themselves in a world of Infinite Giving and where no one member gets exhausted and gives up.

Givers Gain is a great way to live life in general and it is a standard that we can all apply to ourselves—key word being "ourselves"; again, it is not a stick to hit people with who may not adopt the philosophy. There is no measure of Givers Gain, no scoreboard, no points. It's personal to you. All you need to consider is whether your giving feels right to you.

One of the reasons that people give up on the philosophy of giving as a way of life is that they understand how to give, they give so much and so often, and then they exhaust themselves with their giving efforts. If you get exhausted of giving, then your giving stops and Infinite Giving stops. You may be able to recover your giving mojo again and you may not. The 7 Principles when followed correctly allow the world to create Givers Gain Communities that sustain themselves in a world of Infinite Giving and where no one member gets exhausted and gives up.

We recently heard of an example on how Givers Gain had become corrupted. Members of a local business group had started referring to Givers Gain in a transactional way, and they had inadvertently started to talk about Givers Gain as if it were an expectation.

To illustrate: They were saying things like, "BNI is amazing! You give referrals to others, and they give you more business in return." Their point was true, but the impression created for the visitor and other members is that you will get something back (business) if you give something to another member. Purely transactional.

This is further evidenced when you meet with disillusioned

members, who say, "I am not getting as much as I want from my membership." They expected that they would get more in return for their involvement.

When you ask what they did, their response will show why they weren't as successful as others. They did very little except attend the meetings, and even when they did, it was with an attitude of expecting a return. They were embracing only the Gain in Givers Gain.

The best way to think about Givers Gain finally dawned on the leaders of the group. They realized that the most successful participants were those who didn't only measure results they got, they *truly* focused on giving.

They are involved, committed members, who genuinely give. They have a giving strategy. Their conversations are peppered with quality, uplifting words about other members. They look to pass referrals with a genuine attitude of not expecting in return. They may even go several weeks without receiving business, but you would never know it because they don't stop their giving during these personally lean times.

These people are easy to spot because their attitude will be the true beacon.

**True Givers Gain is an intention
and not an expectation.**

You will most likely feel a twinge of envy too, as you learn just how successful they have been within their chosen Givers Gain Community. You will be wondering how they have had so much success because it doesn't seem that they are hogging the limelight or talking about it. They have truly understood Givers Gain.

True Givers Gain is an intention and not an expectation.

Those invested in the process know that they are gaining every time they meet, every leadership role that they occupy, every time they encourage someone else to stay the course. Their businesses will be growing, their influence expanding, and their results will be worthy of emulating.

Find these people, stay close to them, catch their spirit of Givers Gain, and live by the 7 Principles. We promise you it will be worth your while! Only when you apply all the principles are you truly living a life of Givers Gain and on the path of Infinite Giving.

CHAPTER 7

PRINCIPLE 3, GIVE
MORE THAN EXPECTED

In the time of mass production, with same-day deliveries and instant purchasing, doing what you say you were going to do is simply no longer enough to leave a lasting impression on those around us. We must always look for and take advantage of any given situation to exceed expectations.

Here is a brilliant example of how a member of staff from a British supermarket recognized and took advantage of an opportunity to exceed a customer's expectation and how, in the true spirit of Givers Gain, it came back to them tenfold.

A confused three-and-a-half-year-old Lily Robinson looked upon a loaf of recently purchased bread and asked her mother, "Why do they call it tiger bread when it looks like a giraffe?"

In Lily's mind, the broken crust on the bread was a much closer match to the patches on a giraffe than the stripes of a tiger.

"Why don't you write and ask them?" replied her mother. This is a standard response for a parent bombarded with questions, and as many parents know, it normally does the job in ending the line of interrogation.

However, Lily was determined to find out the reason behind the name and with the help of mom and dad, set about writing her letter to the supermarket's customer service team.

[See photo below]

Dear

Sainsssssssssssssssssssssssbbbbbbbbbbbbburyyys,

Why is tiger bread c\alled tiger bread?
It should be c\alled giraffe bread.

Love from Lily Robinson 3 ½

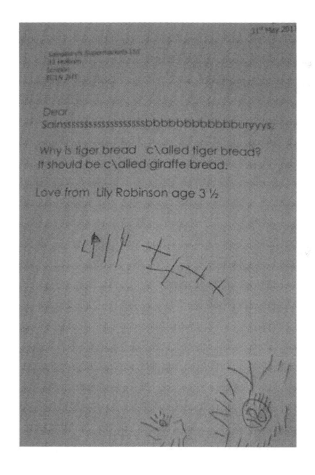

55

Above is a direct transcript of the typed letter which was signed by Lily with four kisses and a drawing of what looks like a chicken and an angry fried egg.

Placed in an envelope and sent to the head office of the supermarket chain, Lily's mother expected that to be the end of the story. To everyone's surprise, customer support manager Chris King wrote back.

Dear Lily,

Thanks so much for your letter. I think renaming tiger bread giraffe bread is a brilliant idea—it looks much more like the blotches on a giraffe than the stripes on a tiger—doesn't it.

It's called tiger bread because the first baker who made it a looong time ago thought it looked stripy like a tiger. Maybe they were a bit silly.

I really liked reading your letter so I thought I would send you a little present.

I've put a £3 gift card in with the letter, if you ask your mum or dad to take you to Sainsbury's you could use it to buy some of your own tiger bread (and maybe if mum and dad says it's OK you can get some sweeties too!). Please tell an adult to wait 48 hours before using this card.

I'm glad you wrote in to us and hope you like spending your gift card. See you in store soon.

Yours Sincerely

Chris King (age 27 & 1/3)
Customer Manager

Enclosed £3 gift card"

So impressed was Lily's mother with the warm response, she posted both letters on her blog along with her gratitude for the effort shown by a large corporation to respond to a little girl. Before long, the exchange between Lily and Chris had gone viral and a campaign with over 1,000 comments was started to lobby Sainsbury's to change the name officially from Tiger to Giraffe bread.

Spotting a unique opportunity to reinforce the "customer is always right mantra," leadership approved the name change. Placed on the shelf where the now correctly named Giraffe bread sits, reads a sign: "Thanks to a clever suggestion from one of our customers we've changed the name of our tiger bread to giraffe bread. Don't worry, the recipe hasn't changed and the bread still tastes as great as ever."

There are many ways of exceeding expectations and this example gives us just a few of those. Sainsbury's did many things right.

An employee not only took the time to respond in kind to the initial letter but also bestowed a small but unexpected gift on the customer. Sainsbury's also demonstrated a company culture of being willing to listen to the feedback of the client-base and, finally, and sometimes the most impactful, the communications from the company showed soul and a sense of humor. These tiny and often overlooked points turned a retail giant into a local shop in the eyes of thousands.

As demonstrated above, the ability to exceed is very rarely financial. We get multiple quotes, use comparison websites, and drill down suppliers for the very best price so when a delivery is made or a job completed it is the addition of the "intangible" that helps to surpass our expectations. Here are other ways you can go above and beyond.

- Rearranging your schedule to ensure a customer's changing deadline is hit.

- Asking for, listening to, and actioning genuine feedback once a job is complete, and telling your customer that they have had an impact.

- Including a small gift with each delivery.

- Sending a personalized note thanking the customer for their order.

- Calling an existing customer just to "check in."

The opportunities are plentiful to exceed your customers' current expectations. Are you doing them all? In fact, are you doing any?

Finally, and somewhat strangely, one action above all others—and consistently over time—will ensure a customer's expectations are exceeded. What is that action you might wonder? It is to say sorry when something goes wrong and work tirelessly to make it right.

Miscommunications happen in business, deliveries go

missing, proofs are misread, and incorrect products are dispatched. It's not whether something will go wrong but rather how we deal with them when they do that counts. This is all about service recovery.

The default position in most businesses is to attribute blame: to suppliers, to couriers, to other departments, and sometimes even to the customer themselves. The best step you can ever take is admit that something has gone wrong, apologize, and then ask how you can make it right. This "grown up" approach will actually strengthen your relationship and ensure that your client feels valued and respected.

At the point when an unhappy customer walked into your premises or picked up the phone, they were expecting a fight. Their best-case scenario was securing a replacement of the order or service after the expecting to spend much emotion.

By instantly "losing" the argument and putting the focus on customer satisfaction, you have done more than they were hoping for. Dale Carnegie was correct:

> You can't win an argument. You can't because if you lose it, you lose it; and if you win it, you lose it.
>
> Why? Well, suppose you triumph over the other man and shoot his argument full of holes and prove that he is *non compos mentis*. Then what? You will feel fine. But what about him? You have made him feel inferior. You have hurt his pride. He will resent your triumph.

When people exceed expectations, exciting things can happen. Excitement is contagious, and you enter a spiral of success. We can look to a UK-based charity to see this in greater detail.

Lisa Ellams is the founder of Cystic Fibrosis Supporters Bromley, UK. Two years ago, she received an invitation to a local business meeting, to meet local business owners who would want to help to get her cause off of the ground.

She attended a meeting expressing that her organization needed three trustees, legal help to obtain a charity number, donations to open the first charity shop in England for Cystic Fibrosis, oh, and a shop.

Lisa explained that the money raised would go in part to the much-needed medical research to continue the fight against the disease. The charity would also help many Cystic Fibrosis Warriors at the children's ward at a local hospital.

The group embraced Lisa as one of the family, going above and beyond to help make her charity a success. She now has four trustees, a charity number, and three storage units with donations and shop fittings. Equally exciting, the first ever shop is scheduled to open.

Lisa gave back to the business group by using social media to attract new clients for her Givers Gain Community, her BNI group. On average she brought two new businesses to meet the group every week. Some of these businesses became clients, trusted suppliers and collaboration partners for the very people who were helping her charity. This is exactly how Givers Gain works to drive Infinite Giving.

Lisa said, "Without the support of that local BNI business group, Cystic Fibrosis Supporters would not exist. With like-minded and passion driven people backing you, many people's lives can change."

As somewhat of a side note, one of the authors of this book voluntarily had his chest waxed to raise money for Lisa's charity; we'll let you decide which one.

It only ever takes a little time and effort to really set you apart from the rest.

Exceeding expectation can be achieved at every stage of your relationship, and the wonderful thing about this principle is that it only ever takes a little time and effort to really set you apart from the rest.

CHAPTER 8

PRINCIPLE 4, GIVE WHAT YOU CAN AFFORD

Giving more than expected (the previous chapter) and giving what you can afford are not contradictory or mutually exclusive. This is part of applying discernment to your actions. Give more than you may be expected to, but never exceed what you can afford. Do one, while respecting the other.

In a tweet from June 19, 2019, the wonderful author and motivational speaker Lisa Nichols wrote, "Your job is to fill your own cup, so it overflows. Then you can serve others, joyfully, from your saucer." This tweet reinforces her teachings that we should give to others from our saucer, which is in turn filled by our overflowing cup.

The focus on protecting ourselves first will ensure that our giving activities are sustainable and enjoyable over a long period of time. No one wants to feel like helping others is an exhausting chore. While some people may stick at it for a while, unless we experience an emotional pay off, most will give up in the mid- to long-term.

For some giving activities, it is obvious when we need to stop. Money, for example, is a finite resource. Of course, we can always make more. But, at the time of giving, we can only gift so much without generating a negative impact on our own life and the lives of those we support.

It's when we get to the less tangible resources that we really need to pay attention: time, energy, emotion, influence, and knowledge. These are all harder to quantify than money, and an over-gifting of these can have an even more damaging effect on your personal well-being. However, these intangible resources can be the most impactful: "For me, when belief in myself was, and sometimes still is, hard to find, others who I admired and respected freely gave their belief in me. So, did it have a transformational effect? Absolutely, without Givers Gain, I wouldn't be where I am today!!" This statement came from our friend Tara Schmakel when we asked her about Givers Gain. Tara added:

As a timid but driven individual who worked alone mostly, I wasn't always confident in speaking or taking a leadership role within my chapter and eventually the region. I often felt intimidated by certain people or professions and felt insignificant as I did self-comparisons. Being a part of BNI built my confidence because as I helped the members of my chapter, others began helping and supporting me. They complemented my efforts and gave me positive feedback as well as helpful guidance. As I grew, they celebrated my successes with me. The positivity and support I received gave me an internal nudge to do more and to stretch my comfort zone until it had expanded well beyond what I would have ever imagined."

Her experience shows the transformational effect that can

be achieved, when, if used correctly, that support and encouragement can be life-changing. We only have a finite amount of energy and we must ensure that those we give to are worthy recipients. We must, protect our own vital resources.

Tara admits, "As an introvert, I have learned that I need to actively protect my own energy when giving of time and energy to others by taking time to refuel and recharge."

If we give too much to others without allowing ourselves to be "refilled", we will drop out of Infinite Giving all together. In contrast, there are people whose cup is positively gushing into their saucer and flowing out all over the floor. These people are so guarded with their resources that they give only after they have received. This is not Givers Gain.

To illustrate where this giving sweet spot is, we use the concept called flow. Flow is where people are challenged and energized by the task at hand. They thrive in the moment and enjoy the planning, process, and outcome of the activity.

When does flow happen? It happens when their ability and the difficulty of the task have met perfectly. They are not overqualified or have too many skills and get bored as a result. Nor are they lacking in the required ability, drowning and panicking about failing. We have all seen people who have been promoted above their competence. When the activity is neither too easy nor too hard for people to perform, they are "in flow."

This concept applies perfectly when we look at giving. Effective members of the Givers Gain Communities will protect their own reserves so not to drain themselves and will also immediately help others when they recognize that they have an excess.

This perfect flow of giving makes it both rewarding and sustainable. We can see this through an example in India.

Jadav Payeng who lives on Majuli in Assam, India, the world's largest river island, was alarmed at the young age of 16 by the devastation caused to his home following extreme flooding and subsequent drought. He earned a small income by selling the milk of his cows to the local villages and had very little time or money to rectify the damage that he saw. He did, however, understand that the roots of trees and plants kept the island together. So, in 1979 and in a bid to prevent further erosion to his homeland, he decided he would plant a sapling in the barren soil every day for the foreseeable future.

In 2009 photojournalist Jitu Kalita hired a boat to take pictures of birds around the Brahmaputra River, which flows around Majuli Island. While paddling through the shallows he saw something strange. It looked like a forest in the distance:

"I began walking towards it" Jitu said, "and when I reached it, I couldn't believe my eyes. I had found a dense forest in the middle of a wasteland."

Thirty-nine years after that original commitment to plant a

sapling every day, Jadav has created a woodland that covers 1,360 acres and is now home to Bengal tigers, rhino, vultures, and 115 elephants.

Jadav gave what he could afford. Having very little time or money, he committed to a small act daily that has compounded over time to produce something breath taking. The father of three, now in his late 50s, says he will continue to plant until his last breath and goes to his "special forest" daily to continue his work. His ultimate goal is for his forest to spread over 5,000 acres.

In a wonderful example of Infinite Giving, the spread of the forest has sped up as the trees are now self-seeding, and Jadav describes his self-made home as "pretty blissful, with little stress."

Give what you can afford, give with consistency, and, like Jadva, be prepared to benefit from your own activities. We've seen people give and give from their cup, but it's not a long-term strategy for success.

The fact is, Infinite Giving is truly a marathon of an endeavor—it's most definitely not a sprint. We have met so many people who practice what we call "hyperactive giving," and they mistakenly approach it at the speed of an all-out sprint. They want to be absolutely everywhere and meet everyone and they go, go, go ALL of the time, until they soon inevitably burn out, "collapse," and give up.

It's a real shame because if these people would, from the beginning, just slow down and take the time to develop a giving strategy and understand that it takes time, patience, hard work, dedication, commitment, and endurance, they would be reaping great rewards from their efforts instead of exhausting themselves with nothing to show for it in the end.

Infinite Giving, at its core, is about taking the time to create something genuine, whether it be a tropical forest planted over decades or a trusted relationship with a family member, friend, client or supplier. Each will take effort, dedication, and consistency to flourish.

Many confuse commitment with activity, and sure, activity is important, but without building trust right along with it, activity won't get you very far in the long run. You can run around all day long going to events, shaking people's hands, but if you're not spending time following up and developing your relationship with the people you meet, then your giving will potentially be ineffective and misguided.

**Do not confuse activity
with accomplishment.**

Unless you take time to understand those who you are giving to, their needs, motivations, and desires before you give, you won't really achieve much of anything. Your activities will not lead to long-term results, and your efforts and energy will be wasted. Do not confuse activity with accomplishment.

The goal here is to give what we can afford and make sure what flows into our saucer is distributed effectively to those that need and deserve it. Ultimately, we must practice discernment with that which we can afford.

Give from your saucer, not your cup.

By understanding that giving is a long-term strategy, it will always allow us to recharge and refill. Give from your saucer, not your cup.

CHAPTER 9

PRINCIPLE 5, IT'S OK TO GAIN

Right at the heart of Infinite Giving is the philosophy of Givers Gain. Remember the second word, Gain. Givers Gain is two words and receiving is part of the philosophy. Being a good receiver of a gift is vital to ensure the philosophy works and that it leads to a life of Infinite Giving.

Givers Gain is two words and receiving is part of the philosophy.

Without accepting that it is OK to gain, a giver will soon find themselves out of resources and giving will stop. It is vital that the great givers also gain what they need so that they can give over and over. In that way, Infinite Giving becomes a part of who they are and how they act daily.

Many people talk about the concept of "you only get out what you put in." This is often true of gaining within the philosophy of Givers Gain. Giving first is fundamental. But, you cannot constantly give at your own expense.

The story of Brenda Jones illustrates this point beautifully. In 2016, Brenda Jones was a 69-year-old great-grandmother who had spent a long year on the donor list waiting to receive a liver. On July 18, a hospital in North Texas called—they had a viable liver for her. It was the call she and her family had been waiting for; there was hope.

Meanwhile, 23-year-old Abigail Flores had a crisis situation, and she had suffered complete liver failure. She also needed a liver and only had hours to live. Her situation was more urgent than Brenda's. Without a transplant, doctors feared Abigail had maybe one more day to live. The transplant surgeon Dr. Greg McKenna called Brenda and asked her if she would give up her donor organ to save the life of this young woman.

Brenda agreed to give the organ to Abigail. She said of the gift, "In my heart, I wouldn't have been able to live with the liver if I had let this little girl die. I just knew this is what I had to do."

Brenda was placed back at the top of the donor list and got a new liver just four days later. Both women recovered together in the same ward.

There will always be people who need a new liver, yet Brenda gave away her first chance for what she saw as the greater good. This does not mean, however, that she needed to sacrifice her own life and pass up every opportunity offered to her. It was right for her to accept the second transplant and the new lease of life that came along with it.

It is OK to accept and create opportunities to gain provided you are an equal part of the Givers Gain Community. If you have put in, then it's right that you should take out. Indeed, even if you have not put in then sometimes you just have to fill your cup so that it may overflow into your saucer as discussed in the previous chapter.

This is the way Givers Gain works. We must be receptive to

gaining. Even the biggest of givers need to gain from time to time. One tendency when you are a giver is to push people away saying, "It's OK," I do not need help. This can come over as not wanting to impose or, more dangerously interpreted, that you are in some way superior to others in your community.

One tendency when you are a giver is to push people away.

We recently heard a wonderful example of a local businessman, Phil, who had taken responsibility for a networking group. He stood up at each meeting and shared his knowledge and experience with the members with the goal of helping them grow both the size of their group and in turn, and more importantly, their revenue for their business.

After a few visits, a member approached Phil, thanked him for all he was doing, and asked him what he could do to assist Phil in growing his own business. Phil graciously declined the offer of help, stating that he was "only there to help the group."

Phil turned up regularly and was successful in helping the members increase their return from the group and in introducing new members to their network. However, after each time, he was approached by the same member with the simple request,

"How can I help?" and each time, Phil batted off the request with a smile.

On the fourth time of asking, however, and after delivering his standard response, Phil was shocked when the member lost his temper and said, "Well, if I'm not good enough to help, forget you!" (He may or may not of used the word forget.)

With Givers Gain, we all have the right to give AND to gain.

Phil had tried to be the ultimate giver, but what he didn't realize that he was robbing someone else of the gift of giving by refusing to accept help and GAIN. Givers Gain is two words and they are as important as one another.

With Givers Gain, we all have the right to give AND to gain.

Sometimes we don't want to be a burden or appear vulnerable in front of our peers. The fact is, in a room full of people, there will always be some who are growing, some who are successful, and there will definitely be those who are facing challenge. We know it is better to face challenges together. The confidence to be vulnerable comes from building trust within a team or a group. When trust is high and strong, then people are more willing to ask for the help they need. Building trust in your network is a key strategy to unlock the power of the gain side of Givers Gain.

The confidence to be vulnerable comes from building trust within a team or a group.

Our experience is that people can be very uncomfortable about seeking gain. They believe that Givers Gain is all about giving and that the gaining should not ever cross their mind. This is an understandable thought process; however, it is also all part of the philosophy to ask your community for support when you need it and be open to gaining as much as you are to giving.

If you do not get this right, then eventually you will be running on empty and you will drop out of your Givers Gain Community. We should only be giving the "excess" of what we have available, and at the same time by gaining, you refill your reserves and allow others the opportunity to experience the gift of giving.

We are often too busy in our own routines to recognize when others are experiencing "pain." This oversight is not through neglect or an unwillingness to assist. It is simply because sometimes life gets in the way.

Ask for what you need and not what you think the community can provide.

The fact is that in high-trust groups people are very willing to work with you on what you need. We suggest that when the time is right you should ask for what you need and not what you think the community can provide.

This is illustrated by Andy's story. Andy spent two years in his BNI group, giving thoughtful referrals, doing the one-to-ones and not always feeling much return. He knew the group trusted him and he got the odd referral here and there. The problem was that he was simply not being clear in what he wanted to gain from his group and membership.

He got to a point where his business was at make or break time ... so he stood up and asked the room for help. He said, "I want to be here; I want to succeed, and I could really use all of your help to get there. I have three months to turn things around otherwise I'll have to leave and seek employment." Within an hour he had referrals and, more importantly, ideas and feedback.

When you've built a meaningful relationship, you've earned the right to ask.

Six months later, his business model changed (thanks to a member's advice). He now has regular repeat referrals from all of the business community, and he now asks for what he wants.

When you've built a meaningful relationship, you've earned the right to ask.

The responsibility is on us to ask for assistance when needed.

CHAPTER 10

PRINCIPLE 6, STAY HUMBLE

Humble people don't think less of themselves; they just think of themselves less.

Some of the most accomplished people we know are humble. In fact, many of the most successful people we've ever met have been remarkably humble. We believe that being humble and being successful don't have to be mutually exclusive.

Humble people don't think less of themselves; they just think of themselves less.

Here's a story from Ivan's past. Ivan remembers going to a political function in his late teens. He had decided that he wanted to pour himself into a campaign for a particular individual whose platform he appreciated. Then ... he met him.

They were introduced by someone high up in the candidate's campaign. As soon as the politician learned that Ivan was a lowly college student, he immediately lost interest. His eyes were darting across the room looking for someone more successful than Ivan. He ended up being very dismissive and came across incredibly arrogant.

After that encounter, Ivan decided not to help in his campaign. Instead, he picked someone running for a different office. This person was engaging and friendly. He was respectful with people who didn't "appear" to have much to offer. He spoke with everyone, rich or poor, educated or uneducated, young or old. He welcomed Ivan's involvement in the campaign with enthusiasm.

Within six months, Ivan ended up running his entire regional campaign office. He willingly put in hundreds of hours in that campaign and helped this person win office. This experience taught Ivan a lot about the kind of leader he wanted to be as he became more successful in life.

A humble person's ego does not enter the room before they do.

Humility costs nothing but yields amazing returns. Being humble sounds simple enough, but what does that actually look like? There are many things that can help someone show their humility. Here is a list of a few that we think are important.

1. A humble person's ego does not enter the room before they do.
2. They are approachable, meaning that they are friendly and easy to talk to.
3. They listen and ask questions during a conversation.
4. They maintain eye contact in a conversation and stay engaged in the discussion. They show genuine interest.

5. They are comfortable making people feel at ease and thanking people when appropriate.

6. Humble individuals tend to have an "abundance mentality" and they tend to focus on solutions rather than simply rail about problems.

7. They are situationally aware and have strong emotional intelligence.

8. They are not self-absorbed. They know their strengths and are comfortable with who they are, but they don't behave as though the world revolves around them.

9. Most importantly, they regularly practice Givers Gain. They approach life with a certain amount of altruism and strive to make a difference for others.

As we become more successful in life, it's critical to maintain one's humility. We've all met people who behave in a pompous manner and generally expect to be the center of attention most of the time. In the long run, we don't believe this serves people well.

One of the world's most beloved billionaires, Richard Branson, holds this regard not because of his extensive charity work or his quirky marketing tricks, but because he remains humble at every opportunity. Speak to almost any member of the Virgin organization who has met him and they will tell you how amazing he is to work for.

Ivan has had several opportunities to visit Richard on Necker Island, his private island in the Caribbean. On one of those visits, Richard asked everyone if they wanted to visit the island he had just purchased next to Necker. Of course, everyone said yes. The next day he walked a small group of people around the island showing them the sights. As they were wrapping up the tour, the group walked by a small house that was being knocked down by two local workers with sledgehammers. This was clearly back-breaking work. Rather than just walk on by, Richard excused himself and approached the two men. He said hello to the man he knew and introduced himself to the second individual. Richard then went on to tell the worker about his plans for the island. He told the man that he recognized this was hard work, but it was critical to his overall plan. He went on to say that when this house came down, he'd be able to bring in equipment to dredge out the little bay next to the house. Then they could bring in heavy equipment to start to build the roads and the homes that would were planned for the island. Richard pointed out where the tennis courts would go, where the common areas would be built, and where the water sports would be located. Richard ended the conversation by saying that he appreciated the worker's efforts because his vision for the island could only take place after this house came down. Everything else was dependent on that job, and he thanked the two of them for their work and came back to the group touring the island.

What humility. Here was a billionaire who took a few moments of his time to tell the equivalent of a Virgin Island's minimum wage day laborer his vision for the island and why the man's work was integral to the overall plan. Some individuals we've met wouldn't give this man the time of day. Branson gave him his big vision for the island, which all started with the work he was doing.

Humility like this is powerful and inspirational, and this isn't the only time Ivan has seen this. About a year later, Richard walked into a large event for his newly launched Virgin Galactic company. As he walked into the house where the event was being held, there were hundreds of people waiting to meet him. As he entered the foyer, he noticed two house staff who were leaning up against the wall in awe of the billionaire walking into the great room. He stopped in front of the two ladies and spent a few moments thanking them for all the work they were doing to make this event a success. He told them that this was an important event for him and he appreciated their efforts. These ladies weren't even employed by Richard. They worked for the man who owned the house, but Richard made sure to take the time to edify them for their contributions to his event. This is humility in action.

No one is perfect with this all the time. The process is a journey, not a destination. It is something we must always strive for. At large events, we know that we've had a good day when people say to us that they are surprised at how easy we are to talk to or that they felt that we came across like a "regular person." We believe that there is a "regular person" in all of us. Showing that person to others is part of being humble.

If you achieve success in business, strive to shatter people's expectations and demonstrate real humility. Be someone who is engaging and caring as well as knowledgeable and successful.

Above all, **remember that humble people don't think less of themselves, they just think of themselves less.**

CHAPTER 11

PRINCIPLE 7, THE GRATITUDE EFFECT

We recognize that when some people hear the phrase an "Attitude of Gratitude," they are going to think, *"Yeah, yeah, yeah, more new-age psychobabble, but we want hard facts."* Well, we agree that hard facts are important and here are some from reputable sources who argue convincingly about the science of gratitude's positive impact.

- Harvard Medical School recently reported that there have been multiple studies showing that people who express gratitude are "more optimistic and felt better about themselves."

- The Templeton Foundation conducted studies that showed that an "attitude of gratitude" can actually have a positive and "lasting effect on the brain."

- A paper published by the Yale Center for Emotional Intelligence concluded that "expressing gratitude completes [a] feeling of connection" with others (something we'd say is vital in building relationships).

- Neuroscientists argue that gratitude is effective. Paul Zak, professor at Claremont Graduate University states, "the neuroscience shows that recognition has the largest effect on trust." This is especially the case when it's tangible, unexpected, personal, and public.

- University of California – Berkley researchers conducted fMRI scans on individuals who wrote gratitude letters and compared them to the fMRI scans of people who did not. They found that the people who wrote gratitude letters had a greater activation in the medial prefrontal cortex than those who did not write the letters. The medial prefrontal cortex is, among other things, believed to be an area of the brain that triggers responses to nicotine, drugs, and alcohol. In other words, showing gratitude is proven to be a healthy way of getting high.

- Studies by the Cicero Group that were published in *Forbes* found that people who are on the receiving end of gratitude have a 33% increase in their innovation, a 22% increase in work results, and they stay with the organization longer than those who are in companies who do not have a practice of appreciating their people.

**The gratitude effect is not
new-age; it's science.**

So much for psychobabble. Gratitude improves attitude, feelings of connection, and results. The gratitude effect is not new-age; it's science.

Gratitude works when someone is coming from a place of being grateful and acknowledging people along the way. This means that it is important to take time to notice all the good things you might take for granted. Gratitude, like so many other principles of success, is simple, but not easy, meaning that this is a simple concept—but it is not an easy concept to apply regularly in your life. It's not easy, because the easy thing is to notice what is wrong, what you don't like, what annoys you, or the problems that you face.

Gratitude, like so many other principles of success, is simple, but not easy.

There are many different ways that people keep track of the positive things in their lives. Some keep a daily gratitude journal while others vocalize the things they are grateful for before the evening meal or during their morning routine to start the day off in the right mindset. One of our authors builds a "Thank You" list. When the opportunity presents itself, he spends time phoning each name and giving the gratitude that is rightly deserved.

These activities can help people focus on what is going right in their lives as opposed to all of the other "stuff" that gets in the way. These practices can be transformative.

The gratitude effect requires a life-long journey of developing our ability to be grateful.

What we have learned over the years is that if you focus on problems then you become a world-class expert at problems, and it is hard to show gratitude when you are obsessed with the problems around you. However, if you focus on solutions, you can become a world-class expert at solving those problems. This process begins by recognizing what is right around us. From that starting point we can be grateful for those elements and begin to acknowledge those around us for the efforts they are making. The gratitude effect requires a life-long journey of developing our ability to be grateful.

Expressing gratitude completes the feeling of connection with others. Here is how you can start this practice today: Many people have helped us during our lifetime. They are "in our story." Have you acknowledged them? Have you thanked them? Have you recognized the difference they have made for you?

We recently heard a story from a woman whose 16-year-old son was attending school irregularly, his grades began to fail, and he started drinking alcohol. Worst of all, he was caught stealing a car and joy riding late at night. She told us that he was making some really poor life decisions and that she was beside herself with what to do.

She decided to send him to a leadership conference to see if that would help take his life in a new direction. At first, he declined but around the holidays, he said that if this was that important to her, he "would do it for her."

The gratitude effect doesn't take much effort and costs little or nothing.

He attended the multi-day event and came home telling her that the event was amazing. He learned that people matter. Decisions matter. The people around you matter. She told us that one of the speaker's at that event had a particularly large impact on the young man. She then reached out to the speaker from that event and told him the story. She expressed her gratitude for the impact that his talk had on her son's life. She told him, "You gave me my son back." The speaker was so moved that he sent a video message to the young man telling him how grateful he was that he said something that the boy found helpful and that he was proud to be a small part of that. What's more, the young man replied and told him a little about the life that he was now creating for himself.

The gratitude effect doesn't take much effort and costs little or nothing, yet it makes a difference in yourself and the people around you. When you acknowledge people in this way, people are drawn to you like a magnet because it accelerates the relationship building process.

As the story above shows, the gratitude effect can come full circle and then continue to spiral off in new, impactful directions. Believe us. It's science.

CHAPTER 12

APPLYING GIVERS GAIN IN YOUR BUSINESS

Givers Gain is not only a great way to get business; it's an even better way to do business. How you use Infinite Giving as described in this book and the principles of Givers Gain in your business will depend on where you feel you are on your journey to success.

Givers Gain is not only a great way to get business; it's an even better way to do business.

Giving has many cultural and legal differences around the world. In some cultures, giving is seen negatively, yet throughout this book we have addressed how Infinite Giving is a positive force in society and that this can be applied in every business regardless of location or culture.

What is important in acts of giving is our motivation. Here is a list of motivations that fits with the philosophy of Givers Gain and helps us main mental clarity around our motivations when we give.

1. We give because we understand that in a community, what we do, others will do, and we all benefit.

2. We give because we know that in the same situation others would do the same for us.

3. We give because we want to give back where we have profited before.

4. We give because when we work together, we get bigger and better results than working on our own.

5. We give because we enjoy it.

Having ethical motivation is key to Infinite Giving. You can always give once and justify your motivation, but giving over and over again requires a motivation that is understood not only by you but also by the people you surround yourself with. Adopting one or more of the motivations above will help you stay grounded to your motivation.

Just imagine a world where all business adopted Infinite Giving using the 7 Principles of Givers Gain. Where all businesses had a philosophy of Givers Gain and all of the employees, clients, and suppliers of that company embraced Givers Gain as well. Can you imagine living in a world like that? What would it look like? What problems could Givers Gain solve?

Here are some examples of where giving in business changed lives.

Allen B. is a commercial real estate agent in Orange County, California, USA. He was in BNI around the time of the 2008 recession. Ironically, he said that he had his best year ever during this time.

Throughout 2009 and 2010, Allen had met with as many businesspeople as he possibly could, using the BNI network to find these people and to book a meeting with them. They were not just from his local group but were members throughout the county. The more people he met, the more he was able to become a super connector for the local business community. He was generating a ton of business for the local economy simply by making connections and giving the gift of a referral.

He even won awards for it and became the star of his group. He was recognized as having the most one-to-ones, and he also gave out the most referrals. Allen focused on building relationships and once he was convinced he had found a good business opportunity for both of his contacts he would often phone the contact on the spot and put them together, thus creating a powerful introduction much more likely to lead to business.

When asked how all of this activity had affected his business at a bad time for real estate, he said, "I am completing the best year in my 26 years in the business. I have had a great, great year."

What is amazing about this story is that it happened at a time when businesses were dealing with a massive recession and the fallout from that recession. More importantly, Allen was in a business that was hit as hard or harder than the overall majority. Through the power of Givers Gain and a mindset of Infinite Giving, Allen had his best year ever.

Giving in business as in life works in many different ways. Here is another example.

Have you ever met a person who embodies most, if not all of the 7 Principles of Givers Gain and is living Infinite Giving? We have, and his name is David Spragg.

David runs a fantastic print business. He offers a brilliant service, great value, and delivers when he says he will, if not before. If you ever try to pay him a compliment, he'll offer a sheepish smile and an explanation that he was only "doing his job."

Just up the road from where his business is based is the area's largest independent hotel, which, of course, he is a trusted supplier for. After turning around an order on a particularly short deadline, the hotel manager, showing the gratitude effect, offered David a meal for two at the hotel's restaurant as a way of saying thank you.

David thanked his client, graciously declined the offer, and instead asked for something else—for them to take the call of one of his other clients, a commercial designer and project manager named Suzanne. Suzanne had recently asked for help and David, being a supplier of hers, decided to use this opportunity to get her the introduction that her business needed.

The introduction was made, business was done, and both of David's clients were happy.

In the true spirit of Infinite Giving, the additional revenue has allowed Suzanne to take on larger development projects, which David now prints for. The local sub-contractors who are used on these projects have increased revenue and now come to David when they are in need of his products and, due to the quality of his work and products, they become ambassadors and referrers for his business.

Acts of giving change lives.

David is selfless, humble, and a wonderful networker because he embraces the 7 Principles of Givers Gain. The cycle of Infinite Giving continues to benefit him and those around him.

Acts of giving change lives. Acts of giving can be powerful in business regardless of the size.

We can give many things. Here is a list of the types of giving that make a real impact in a business community.

1. Give a referral opportunity between two other businesses you know—maybe a supplier of yours and a client of yours.
2. Give mentoring to a business that needs your expertise.
3. Give your knowledge to local business groups.
4. Give to local education and youth community groups.
5. Give to the elders of the community.

**The more people in the world who
adopt the philosophy of Givers Gain
the more prosperity increases.**

All of this giving activity is part of an eco-system that will come back and benefit you and those you care about in a positive way. You choose how to practice Givers Gain that is right for your business. Once you make a commitment to using the power of Givers Gain to fuel an Infinite Giving strategy for your business, success will follow.

The more people in the world who adopt the philosophy of Givers Gain the more prosperity increases.

The more this happens then the more energy can be given to important global social concerns such as climate change and sustainability of our planet. Infinite Giving allows us to focus on the bigger picture. The bigger picture is living in a world of plenty where resources are plentiful, and the struggle of life is not against each other. Rather, it is against suffering and the sustainability of our planet.

CHAPTER 13

GIVERS GAIN IN EVERYDAY LIFE

Throughout this book we have told stories of exceptional examples of Givers Gain. These examples have illustrated the philosophy of Givers Gain and why it is desirable to get yourself and your business into a state of Infinite Giving. In this chapter, we explore the smaller examples of how people who live Givers Gain in an infinite way.

A bigger difference can be made by people who every day in some small way seek to be kind.

The big gestures are fantastic to hear about and they make a real difference to our society. A bigger difference can be made by people who every day in some small way seek to be kind and give what they can in line with the 7 Principles of Givers Gain.

Let's consider how day-to-day we can make a difference by hearing the short story of our fictional character Jane.

Jane rises early and she always **makes a cup of coffee** *to give to her husband just before she leaves for work. Her husband thanks her and he knows that he will reciprocate late in the day when he will open the red wine for their evening meal.*

Jane heads off to the railway station in her car, and she is conscious to **be considerate** *of the other drivers on the roads that morning. When*

Jane gets to the car park, **she parks away from the main entrance** *knowing that some people are not as mobile as she is, and they will appreciate the spaces nearer to the station.*

The journey into the office is a short one. Today, the train is particularly busy, and Jane **offers her seat** *to an elderly gentleman who got on the train at the last moment. The man thanks her and sits down with an audible sigh of relief.*

When she exits the station, Jane notices a man selling "The Big Issue" (a not-for-profit magazine where all proceeds go directly to the homeless person selling them), **she decides to buys a copy,** *and makes a mental note to save the money spent by not having a mid-morning coffee and replacing it with water. The magazine has some great articles from respected authors, and she remembers how in the past these have helped her both professionally and personally.*

When she arrives at the office as normal, Jane greets everyone warmly. She always asks people how they are and **makes a real effort to listen to the answer.** *Today she spots something in one of the replies and makes a mental note of it.*

Halfway through the morning Bob, a young intern, asks her for some help with a spreadsheet. **Jane helps him** *and afterwards asks Bob* **if he needs any more help.** *It turns out that Bob is really struggling with the company's CRM system. Jane struggled with it herself when the company first introduced it two years ago, and she remembered that her coworker Jim had taken time to help her.* She decided that she could afford the time to sit with Bob just like Jim did with her. *After* an hour Bob thanked her for the amount of time Jane had given him. He even remarked that this had made him feel much better about working for the company.

At lunch Jane seeks out Lucy. She had noticed when she asked Lucy how she was earlier that her reply of "yes fine thank you" had contained more than a little hesitation. **Jane sat with Lucy and listened** as Lucy told of a really tough weekend with her elderly father who was in ill health and needed a lot of looking after. Jane listened as Lucy offloaded about the tough times. Jane took her opportunity to ask Lucy about her father and some of the better times they had shared. Surprisingly, they found out that both of their fathers had played basketball for their college teams and swapped stories about memories their fathers had shared with them. At the end of lunch, Lucy thanked Jane for taking the time to listen and help her remember the good times with her father.

One the way home Jane received a message from Bob saying that today had been the best day he had had working at the company, and he was so excited now he knows how to be more effective.

Jane got home and as she arrived on the drive her next-door neighbor Julie came up to her just as she stepped onto the drive. Julie had a large fruit pie; it was cherry, Jane's favorite. Julie said, "It's yours," thank you so much for looking after our dogs last week. You are an amazing neighbor.

Later that evening her husband passes Jane a glass of wine and they spend the evening watching a great movie after a very unremarkable day for Jane. Jane is happy.

We use this simple story of one person's day to show you how everyday we can live Givers Gain. We have boldened the giving action in one day for Jane. There were many more we could have added, which are simple touches of kindness. We also added elements of the "Gain" for Jane, either during the day or from previous actions—acts of giving that Jane benefited from and memories of gifts that motivated her. Some of Jane's Giving may never be recognized and some may provide a gain in the future. None of this will stop Jane's attitude and her life of Infinite Giving.

Day-to-day when we live in a Givers Gain Community, life is made better for all.

We can all be like Jane and fill our days with both remarkable and unremarkable gifts. Some days these gifts will be bigger than others. Some days we will give and some days we will receive. Our task is not to keep tally; our task is to notice what our society needs from us on a daily basis. Day-to-day when we live in a Givers Gain Community, life is made better for all.

CHAPTER 14

THE ROCK TUMBLER

In the now famous "lost interview" from the Triumph of the Nerds series by Robert X. Cringely for PBS, Steve Jobs told a story about an old man who lived down his street. Steve reminisced about doing casual yard work for him, raking leaves, cutting grass—the standard stuff that earned him a few bucks here and there.

After a while, a friendship grew between these two and one day a young Steve was invited into the man's workshop. The man showed him a homemade rock tumbler, cobbled together out of an old coffee can and drill motor. He told Steve to go out and get a handful of plain old rocks and then put them into the can, with some water and what looked like a squeeze of toothpaste. (It was actually a grit compound.)

They closed the rock tumbler and turned it on. Steve stood their transfixed as this homemade device rattled away on the workbench. The man told Steve that he would have to come back tomorrow because it would take time to achieve a result.

The next day, Steve stood outside of the locked workshop waiting for the man to come and open up. He could faintly hear the device through the locked door.

After what seemed like an age, the man appeared, unlocked the door, and the young boy rushed to the workbench. The man laid out a white cloth, turned off the tumbler, removed the lid, and poured the contents onto the cloth.

The handful of plain old rocks that Steve had put in there

just a day before had been transformed into "amazingly beautiful polished rocks" of all different colors, shapes, sizes, and patterns.

Like the stones in the rock tumbler, the 7 Principles of Givers Gain need to work together and polish each other to make the final sparkling result.

You can imagine that the young boy wanted to rush out, find a couple of big rocks, and throw them into the tumbler, however he was told that it takes a handful of stones, working together, with a little bit of grit and a little bit of time, to achieve these amazing results. Indeed, if you put in one or two big rocks it would break the machine as the big rocks flew from one side to the other.

Like the stones in the rock tumbler, the 7 Principles of Givers Gain need to work together and polish each other to make the final sparkling result. Throwing just one principle into the rock tumbler would break the system.

We have outlined in this book the 7 Principles of Givers Gain and how if you integrate these into your life you can lead a life of Infinite Giving. When systems like this are created, people will often choose which of the principles they like and which they do not. We often do this subconsciously based on our behavioral style. Like all systems, these principles only work at their optimum when they are blended evenly and in the way designed by the creators.

Just imagine if you left out even just one of the principles. Let's take a look at how this would work.

If you left out **Principle 1 – Are They in Your Light?** You could end up giving in areas of your life where people do not share your values and are not committed to your Givers Gain Community. Over time you would get disillusioned about spreading yourself so thin, and you may well give up on the philosophy of Givers Gain and thus break the system of Infinite Giving.

If you left out **Principle 2 – Give Without Expectation.** Your network will feel that your giving is transactional, breaking down the depth of the relationships that are at the core of Givers Gain.

If you left out **Principle 3 – Give More Than Expected.** People may feel that you are only prepared to meet the minimum standard all the time, and their enthusiasm for the relationship will be less. Thus, you would reduce the impact of Givers Gain.

If you left out **Principles 4 – Give What You Can Afford.** You may well deplete your resources if you start to give from your cup. This deficit will reduce your ability to give and, left unchecked, will result in a downward spiral that leaves you empty and with nothing to offer. If you have an overflowing saucer and fail to engage with giving activities, then the community over time will become aware and disillusioned with your contribution, which will break down the cycle of giving.

If you left out **Principle 5 – It is OK to Gain.** You will be a fantastic Giving Warrior, but over time your ability to give will be diminished. Also, you and those around you will start to question why you are giving so much and not allowing yourself to gain. Eventually this will lead to a lack of care for your community, and you will drop out disillusioned and spent.

If you left out **Principle 6 – Stay Humble.** You will be seen as arrogant in the community and, regardless of your ability to participate, people will not enjoy working with you and will start to favor others instead.

If you left out **Principle 7 – Show Gratitude.** You will be missing one of the most importing elements of the process. People will regard you as ungrateful and not appreciative of the energy they give to your Givers Gain Communities. You may also miss out on the opportunity to develop and strengthen the relationship further.

Imagine a wheel where one of the seven spokes were missing. It would still function in the short term; however, the ride would be bumpy and over time the wheel would break apart and fail. Now imagine if two or more spokes were missing. It would hardly function at all, even in the very shortest of time periods.

It is only when the wheel is complete that it will function perfectly over a long period of time. Remember how all these ideas fit together with this formula:

Infinite Giving can only thrive when all seven principles are applied consistently.

The philosophy of Givers Gain plus the 7 Principles equals Infinite Giving, or:

$$GG + 7P = IG$$

Infinite Giving can only thrive when all seven principles are applied consistently.

CHAPTER 15

GIVERS GAIN IS TRANSFORMATIONAL

Givers Gain is an idea that proclaims we can be something bigger than ourselves.

The world can be a dark and contentious place. War, famine, poverty, hostility, and desperation are all around us. But it doesn't have to be that way. The world can be a better place. We can make a choice—a choice to be a voice of change, a change that can transform the world we live in.

Givers Gain is an idea that proclaims we can be something bigger than ourselves. It's a reaffirmation that our lives have significant meaning and that, through community, we can be our best selves.

For people who get it, this philosophy unlocks a whole new world of meaning and opportunity. So, our job is to help people "get it." More importantly, we can be intentional about helping people reach that place.

Mahatma Gandhi said, "The best way to find yourself is to lose yourself in the service of others." There is a biological imperative that supports these powerful words. In 2010, *Greater Good Magazine* wrote that the National Institutes of Health found that when people give to others, "it activates regions of the brain associated with pleasure, social connection, and trust, creating a 'warm glow' effect. Scientists also believe that altruistic behavior releases endorphins in the brain, producing the positive feeling known as the helper's high."

Researchers at the University of California – Berkley found that people who volunteered to multiple organizations were "44 percent less likely to die over a five-year period than were non-volunteers," and John Cacioppo, author of *Loneliness: Human Nature and the Need for Social Connection*, says, "the more extensive the reciprocal altruism born of social connection . . . the greater the advance toward health, wealth, and happiness."

Giving is contagious. Conscious giving can be infinite.

There is a profound ripple effect that takes place through the act of consciously practicing the Givers Gain philosophy. We have seen the dramatic impact one person can have on another. We've observed the surging ripple that takes place as an act impacts one person and the next person and the next person, and so on. Within a community or a network, the ripple effect that takes place from this philosophy can influence hundreds and thousands of people. In fact, we believe it can influence the world.

Giving is contagious. Conscious giving can be infinite.

Happiness is found in giving.

There is a Chinese saying: "If you want happiness for an hour, take a nap. If you want happiness for a day, go fishing. If you want happiness for a year, inherit a fortune. If you want happiness for a lifetime, help somebody." For centuries, the greatest thinkers have suggested the same thing: Happiness is found in giving.

The results from this philosophy cannot be observed as a straight line in life. It is a complex zigzag of interconnected relationships that lead to a place of contentment and fulfillment, and it begins with the right mindset. It's about taking off your bib and putting on an apron. It's not about what's in it for you, or how much can you get—it's about serving and helping others in a very conscious way. Not doing so in a way that ignores the fact that there are takers in the world, but in a way that consciously chooses to find your fellow givers in the world. It's easy to be cynical and think that the help you can offer is negligible, but it only takes a small gesture to change someone's life.

**It's about taking off your bib
and putting on an apron.**

As a friend of ours said, "I don't even have to think about it anymore. It is part of my personality now."

We've all had people who are in "our story." They are

116

people that we talk about who have changed our life in some way. However, there is something even more important: The real question is not who's in our story but whose story are we in? Whose life have we made a difference in? This is what creates a meaningful life. It's about being a role model for the people around you.

The real question is not who's in our story but whose story are we in? Whose life have we made a difference in?

We often look at the world and hope that someday things will be different. But as our friend and author Sam Horn says, "someday is not a day of the week." If we wait for someday, we are waiting for others to make the first move.

"Someday" can be today and it can start with us. Today is as good a day as any to be our "someday." We can all make a difference starting today. And that difference starts with a transformational change within us in how we deal with the people around us and the world beyond them.

"Someday" can be today and it can start with us.

In Richard Branson's book, *Finding my Virginity,* he talks about something he calls Circles. He says,

> First of all, draw a small imaginary circle around yourself. Before you can do anything for others, make sure you have the right balance . . . in your own life. Only then can you draw a slightly larger circle around your home that incorporates family, friends and neighbors and even the street outside your home. See how you can make a difference to everyone within that circle . . . If you [are] a small company, draw a circle around the whole street or as much of the local community as you feel you and your team can help. Draw up a list of things that need fixing and set about doing so. If you are a national company, draw a circle around your country and set about tackling some of the bigger issues . . . If every individual and every company draws circles, then soon the circles will overlap and we will together resolve most of the problems in the world.

By ensuring that you have the balance from the start, it will allow you to sustainably scale your Infinite Giving. Just imagine if the whole world embraced the philosophy of Givers Gain— a world where everybody lives the principles each and every day. A world of Infinite Giving: our friends, family, neighbors, employers, business owners, employees, sports figures, politicians (we know that's a stretch), everyone practicing this powerful philosophy. What kind of amazing society could we create with that as a guiding principle?

We would be giving without a transactional expectation, giving to people in all parts of our light appropriately, we would understand that we give what we can afford (from our saucer), and that it's OK to gain in such a society. A humble society where saying thank you is the norm.

You may not make a world of difference, but you can make a difference in the world.

Start small but start today. Begin local but think global. Influence one life and you begin to influence the world. Just start with the person next to you and always remember that

You may not make a world of difference, but you can make a difference in the world.

Now, go out and make a difference in the world, one person at a time.

BNI

BNI, the world's largest business networking organization, was founded by Dr. Ivan Misner in 1985 as a way for businesspeople to generate referrals in a structured, professional environment. The organization, now the world's largest referral business network, has thousands of chapters with hundreds of thousands of members on every populated continent. Since its inception, BNI members have passed millions of referrals, generating billions of dollars in business for the participants.

The primary purpose of the organization is to pass qualified business referrals to its members. The philosophy of BNI may be summed up in two simple words: Givers Gain®. If you give business to people, you will get business from them. BNI allows only one person per profession to join a chapter. The program is designed to help businesspeople develop long-term relationships, thereby creating a basis for trust and, inevitably, referrals. The mission of BNI is to help members increase their business through a structured, positive, and professional word-of-mouth program that enables them to develop long-term, meaningful relationships with quality business professionals.

To visit a chapter near you, contact BNI visit its website at www.bni.com.

BIOGRAPHY
IVAN MISNER, PH.D.

Dr. Ivan Misner is the Founder & Chief Visionary Officer of BNI, the world's largest business networking organization. Founded in 1985, the organization now has roughly 10,000 chapters throughout every populated continent of the world. Each year BNI generates tens of millions of referrals resulting in billions of dollars worth of business for its members.

Dr. Misner's Ph.D. is from the University of Southern California. He is a *New York Times* Bestselling author who has written more than two dozen books including one of his latest books—*Who's in Your Room?* He is also a columnist for Entrepreneur.com and has been a university professor as well as a member of the Board of Trustees for the University of La Verne.

Called the *"Father of Modern Networking"* by CNN and one of the *"Top Networking Experts"* by Forbes, Dr. Misner is considered to be one of the world's leading experts on business networking and has been a keynote speaker for major corporations and associations throughout the world. He has been featured in the *L.A. Times, Wall Street Journal,* and *New York. Times,* as well as numerous TV and radio shows including *CNN,* the *BBC,* and *The Today Show* on *NBC.*

Among his many awards, he has been named *"Humanitarian of the Year"* by the Red Cross and was recently the recipient of the *John C. Maxwell Leadership Award.* He is also proud to be the Co-Founder of the BNI Charitable Foundation. He and his wife, Elisabeth, are now "empty nesters" with three adult children. ***Oh, and in his spare time!!!*** he is also an amateur magician and a black belt in karate.

For more information, go to www.IvanMisner.com.

BIOGRAPHY
GREG DAVIES

Greg knows he has the very best job in the world, in fact he feels slightly embarrassed about calling it a job.

Known as the Storyfella, he uses his passion for telling stories to help businesses and communities thrive, and people overcome limiting beliefs and avoidance behaviors.

After working in both large corporations and owning his own small business, he understands that working hard is sometimes unavoidable and necessary, but says "It's ok as long as we understand *why* we are doing it and we surround ourselves with those people who inspire us to be better, every single day."

A multi-award winning director of BNI, corporate trainer, and international motivational speaker, Greg still finds time to drum whenever the opportunity presents itself and is a not so secret Disney fan, citing the first as the ultimate stress relief and the second as his and his two daughters' happy place.

For more information go to www.TheStoryFella.com.

BIOGRAPHY
JULIAN LEWIS

Julian Lewis is passionate about personal and business success; Julian is a portfolio entrepreneur with businesses interests in companies as diverse as IT Support to Film Making. He is a Founding Partner of the business coaching company Integrus Global and an Executive Director of BNI in the UK.

In 1997 he started his first business and has gone on to start and grow businesses ever since. He continues to coach, mentor, and consult to businesses globally.

He still owns the IT company he started in 1999 and serves as a Non-Executive Director of Bad Blood Films Limited. Since starting his first business he has always had the goal to own five profitable businesses at any one time personally and to influence the success of thousands of others. He achieved his goal of five profitable companies in 2018.

Julian believes that everyone achieves more when they are surrounded by the right people. He works with others to grow and unlock their true potential.

He is mad about rugby union and volunteers to help his local Rugby Club; in his time, he had held many management positions at the club including being Chairman for three years. These days to relax he watches live rugby, cycles with friends, and drinks real ale always brewed local to where he is. Julian is a big fan of France and the French culture, food, and wine, and he visits France at least twice a year.

For more information on Julian, go to www.JulianLewis.biz.

Printed in Poland
by Amazon Fulfillment
Poland Sp. z o.o., Wrocław